SIBI

Raising Healthy Children Void Of Rivalry While Nurturing Sibling Bonds And Creating A Strong Family Foundation

Stephanie Morton

Copyright © 2023 by [Stephanie Morton]

All rights reserved. No part of this book may be reproduced in any form or by any electronic or mechanical means, including information storage and retrieval systems, without written permission from the publisher or author, except for the use of brief quotations in a book review.

This book is a work of nonfiction and any resemblance to people, living or dead, or places, events or locales is purely coincidental. The characters are products of the author's imagination and used fictitiously.

TABLE OF CONTENTS

INTRODUCTION

CHAPTER ONE

  The Far-reaching Effects of Sibling Rivalry

CHAPTER TWO

  The Roots of Rivalry

CHAPTER THREE

  Effective Communication

  The Key to Harmonious Sibling Relationships

CHAPTER FOUR

  Building Strong Bonds

  Nurturing Sibling Relationships That Last a Lifetime

CHAPTER FIVE

CHAPTER SIX

  Sibling Harmony in Practice

  Transforming Theory into Reality: Bringing Positive Change to Life

CHAPTER SEVEN

  Navigating Challenges Along the Way

- Dealing with Age Gaps
- Handling Sibling Conflict
- Addressing Individual Needs

CHAPTER EIGHT

- The Lifelong Benefits of Strong Sibling Bonds

CONCLUSION

INTRODUCTION

In the ever-evolving journey of parenthood, one of the most intricate and delicate dynamics we encounter is the relationship between siblings. As a child counselor with nearly a decade of experience, I've had the privilege of witnessing the profound impact that sibling rivalry can have on the lives of children and their families. My name is Stephanie Morton, and I'm here to guide you through a transformative exploration of a topic that is often overlooked in the realm of parenting – the benefits of raising children without rivalry.

In my years of working with families from all walks of life, one thing has become abundantly clear: every child is unique, and so is their relationship with their siblings. Sibling rivalry, that age-old struggle for parental attention and affection, can sow the seeds of discord that, if left unchecked, can bear fruit for years to come. Yet, by understanding the underlying dynamics and employing effective strategies, we can cultivate a home environment where siblings not only coexist but thrive together.

This book is a culmination of my experiences, observations, and unwavering belief in the power of nurturing sibling bonds. It is a guide for parents, guardians, and caregivers who aspire to create a harmonious family atmosphere where love, understanding, and support flourish.

Inside these pages, you'll discover:

The Far-reaching Effects of Sibling Rivalry: We will delve into the profound and often underestimated consequences that sibling rivalry can have on children's emotional, social, and psychological development. You'll gain insight into the long-term impact it can have on the overall family dynamic.

The Roots of Rivalry: Understanding the underlying causes of sibling rivalry is the first step in addressing it. We'll explore the various triggers and circumstances that can ignite competition and animosity among siblings.

Effective Communication: Communication lies at the heart of any healthy relationship. You'll find practical advice on fostering open and honest dialogues among siblings, enabling them to express their emotions, resolve conflicts, and develop empathy.

Building Strong Bonds: Learn how to create opportunities for your children to connect on a deeper level, encouraging cooperation, teamwork, and a sense of belonging within the family unit.

Parenting Strategies: I will share tried-and-tested strategies that empower you as a parent to foster an environment of love and unity, reducing the likelihood of rivalry and promoting a lifelong bond between siblings.

As we embark on this journey together, my hope is to provide you with the tools and insights you need to raise children who not only love each other but also grow up to become individuals who cherish the unique bond they share with their siblings. By the end of this book, you'll be equipped with a renewed perspective on parenting, one that places nurturing sibling relationships at the forefront of creating a harmonious and loving family.

Join me in this transformative exploration, and together, we'll embark on a path toward creating a home filled with laughter, support, and the enduring strength of sibling love.

> **Being fair and being equal are not the same. Our children's needs may be different so to be fair we may need to treat them differently.**

THE SCIENCE:

Sibling are *natural competitors*. This goes back to evolution: there was a time when siblings literally vied for survival and their survival depended on their caregiver. Therefore, the more connected you were to the caregiver, the greater chance you had of survival. Fast-forward to **now** and our kids are wired to compete with each other for our love and attention.

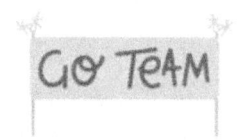

GO TEAM

By putting kids on the **same team** (literally!) we can (temporarily) take competition out of the equation. The more practice our kids have with **collaborating and championing** each other, the more the resentment and jealousy decreases.

CHAPTER ONE
The Far-reaching Effects of Sibling Rivalry

Sibling rivalry, a common and often underestimated aspect of family dynamics, has far-reaching effects that can shape the lives of children and their relationships well into adulthood. Beyond the occasional squabbles and tiffs, sibling rivalry can leave indelible marks on a child's emotional, social, and psychological development.

Emotional Impact: The constant competition for parental attention and affection can create a breeding ground for negative emotions such as jealousy, resentment, and low self-esteem. Children engaged in sibling rivalry may experience feelings of inadequacy or unfulfilled needs, which can lead to emotional turmoil.

Social Consequences: Sibling rivalry can also extend its reach into a child's social life. The animosity and rivalry experienced within the family can manifest in peer interactions, making it difficult for children to build healthy relationships outside the home. This can lead to challenges in making friends, cooperating with others, and resolving conflicts in non-adversarial ways.

Psychological Development: The psychological toll of sibling rivalry can be profound. It can contribute to the development of negative personality traits, such as competitiveness, aggression, or a constant need for validation. In some cases, unresolved rivalry can lead to long-term emotional scars, affecting a person's mental health well into adulthood.

The Ripple Effect on Family Dynamics: Sibling rivalry doesn't just affect the children involved; it can have a ripple effect on the entire family. Parents may find themselves constantly mediating conflicts, leading to stress and strained relationships within the family unit. Moreover, the rivalry can influence how parents perceive and treat their children, inadvertently reinforcing the negative dynamics.

Understanding these far-reaching effects of sibling rivalry is the first step toward addressing and mitigating its impact. By acknowledging the significance of this issue and taking proactive steps to promote healthy sibling relationships, parents and caregivers can help their children grow up in an environment that fosters love, support, and harmonious family bonds.

> **Complimenting them when they treat each other well. Be specific in your praise.**

CHAPTER TWO
The Roots of Rivalry

Sibling rivalry, that age-old phenomenon, often has its roots in a complex interplay of factors within the family. Understanding these underlying causes is crucial to effectively addressing and mitigating rivalry between siblings. In this exploration of the roots of rivalry, we will delve into the dynamics of birth order, jealousy, competition, parental influence, and the triggers that ignite this common familial struggle.

Birth Order and Sibling Dynamics: Birth order, or the order in which siblings are born, plays a pivotal role in shaping sibling relationships. Firstborns may experience the arrival of a younger sibling as a threat to their status as the sole recipient of parental attention. Middle children often grapple with feelings of being overlooked, while youngest children may have a tendency to seek attention by any means necessary. These inherent dynamics can lay the foundation for rivalry as siblings navigate their roles within the family.

Jealousy and Competition: Jealousy is a potent fuel for sibling rivalry. Children, in their quest for affection and approval from their parents, can become intensely jealous of the attention given to their siblings. Whether it's a coveted toy, academic success, or simply the perception of favoritism, jealousy can sow the seeds of rivalry as siblings vie for the same resources – the love and approval of their parents.

Parental Influence: Parents are significant influencers in the development of sibling dynamics. The way parents manage their children's interactions, discipline, and praise can either exacerbate or alleviate rivalry. Unintentional favoritism, even if mild, can trigger feelings of resentment and competition. Conversely, parents who foster an environment of equality and fairness can create a more harmonious atmosphere for their children.

Recognizing Triggers: Sibling rivalry can be triggered by a wide array of circumstances and events. These triggers may include changes in family dynamics, such as the birth of a new sibling, divorce, or the blending of families through remarriage. Stressful life events, academic pressures, or even comparisons made by well-meaning relatives or friends can also ignite rivalry between siblings.

To effectively address the roots of rivalry, parents and caregivers must be attuned to these factors and proactively work to create an environment that fosters cooperation, understanding, and empathy among siblings. It's essential to recognize that rivalry is a natural aspect of sibling relationships, but it can be managed and transformed into a catalyst for growth and lifelong bonds.

In the chapters that follow, we will explore practical strategies for cultivating sibling relationships based on love and support, rather than competition and animosity. By understanding the roots of rivalry and addressing them head-on, we can pave the way for siblings to not only coexist but to thrive together, creating a stronger and more harmonious family unit in the process.

CHAPTER THREE
Effective Communication

Effective communication is the cornerstone of any healthy relationship, and this holds true for the intricate dynamics of sibling relationships. In this chapter, we will explore the vital role that communication plays in nurturing strong, loving bonds between siblings. By learning to communicate openly, honestly, and empathetically, siblings can resolve conflicts, express their emotions, and build connections that endure throughout their lives.

Encouraging Open Dialogue: To foster effective communication among siblings, it is essential to create an environment where open dialogue is not only encouraged but also celebrated. Parents and caregivers can set the stage for this by actively listening to their children, providing a safe space for them to express their thoughts and feelings without judgment.

One effective strategy is to hold regular family meetings where each sibling has the opportunity to voice their concerns, share their experiences, and contribute to family discussions. This practice allows children to feel heard and valued, promoting a sense of belonging within the family unit.

Teaching Conflict Resolution: Conflicts among siblings are inevitable, but they can be valuable opportunities for growth and learning when handled effectively. Teaching children conflict resolution skills is crucial for promoting harmony within the family. Encourage siblings to express their grievances constructively, using "I" statements to express their feelings and needs. For example, "I get angry when you borrow my things without asking" instead "You always take my stuff!"

Furthermore, guide them to actively listen to each other's perspectives. Siblings may not always agree, but understanding each other's viewpoints can help resolve conflicts amicably. Encourage compromise and negotiation, teaching them that solutions can be reached when everyone's needs are considered.

Empathy and Understanding: Empathy is a powerful tool for promoting effective communication. Encourage siblings to put themselves in each other's shoes, helping them understand the emotions and motivations behind their actions. When a child can empathize with their sibling's feelings, they are more likely to respond with compassion and understanding, rather than defensiveness or hostility.

Parents can also model empathetic behavior by demonstrating understanding and patience when mediating conflicts or offering guidance. When siblings witness their parents engaging in empathetic communication, they are more likely to incorporate these skills into their own interactions.

Nurturing Emotional Expression: Effective communication includes the ability to express emotions honestly and appropriately. Encourage children to share their feelings with their siblings, whether they are positive or negative. Teach them that it is okay to feel angry, sad, or frustrated and that expressing these emotions in a healthy way is essential.

Provide siblings with tools for emotional expression, such as journaling, drawing, or simply talking about their feelings. By creating an atmosphere where emotions are acknowledged and validated, parents can help their children develop emotional intelligence and communicate their needs more effectively.

In summary, effective communication is the linchpin of fostering strong, harmonious sibling relationships. Encouraging open dialogue, teaching conflict resolution skills, nurturing empathy and understanding, and promoting emotional expression are all essential components of this process. By providing siblings with the tools and guidance to communicate effectively, parents and caregivers can empower them to build connections that not only endure but also thrive, creating a foundation of love and support that lasts a lifetime.

The Key to Harmonious Sibling Relationships

In the intricate tapestry of family life, sibling relationships are the threads that bind us together from our earliest moments to the milestones of adulthood. These relationships are unique, complex, and enduring, often shaping our identities and influencing our interactions with the world. The key to fostering harmonious sibling relationships lies in understanding the fundamental principles that underpin these bonds.

1. Mutual Respect: At the heart of harmonious sibling relationships is mutual respect. Siblings are individuals with their own thoughts, feelings, and aspirations. Encouraging respect for each other's autonomy and boundaries creates a foundation of trust and cooperation. When siblings respect each other's differences, they can celebrate their uniqueness rather than seeing them as sources of conflict.

2. Effective Communication: Effective communication is the bridge that connects siblings, allowing them to share their thoughts, feelings, and experiences. Encouraging siblings to express themselves openly and honestly helps prevent misunderstandings and fosters empathy. When children feel heard and understood by their siblings, they are more likely to form deep and lasting connections.

3. Conflict Resolution: Conflict is a natural part of any relationship, and sibling bonds are no exception. Teaching children how to resolve conflicts peacefully and constructively is crucial for building harmonious relationships. Conflict resolution skills include active listening, compromise, and finding solutions that meet the needs of all parties involved.

4. Shared Experiences: Creating opportunities for siblings to share positive experiences can strengthen their bonds. Family activities, traditions, and hobbies provide a common ground for siblings to connect, collaborate, and build memories together. These shared moments can serve as a source of joy and support throughout their lives.

5. Parental Guidance: Parents play a pivotal role in shaping sibling relationships. Modeling respect, effective communication, and conflict resolution skills sets a powerful example for children. Additionally, parents can provide guidance and support when conflicts arise, helping siblings navigate challenges and learn from their experiences.

Harmonious sibling relationships are not devoid of disagreements or differences. Instead, they are characterized by a deep sense of connection, love, and support that transcends the challenges of growing up together. By fostering mutual respect, effective communication, conflict resolution skills, shared experiences, and providing parental guidance, siblings can unlock the key to building relationships that enrich their lives and endure the test of time. These relationships become a source of strength, comfort, and companionship that extend far beyond the shared experiences of childhood, leaving a lasting legacy of love within the family.

> **Do not force them to share their belongings or to play with each other. Instead, praise any act of generosity and explain why you like it.**

Spending time separately with each child, to help children connect with you without competing with their siblings.

Getting their ideas about how they can resolve common conflicts.

CHAPTER FOUR
Building Strong Bonds

Siblings are often our first friends, confidants, and companions on the journey of life. Building strong bonds among siblings is not only a gift parents can give to their children but also an investment in the emotional well-being of the entire family. In this chapter, we will explore the importance of cultivating these powerful connections and the practical strategies for doing so.

1. Creating Shared Experiences:

Shared experiences form the cornerstone of sibling relationships. These moments, whether big or small, build a reservoir of shared memories that can be revisited and cherished throughout life. Family vacations, holiday traditions, or even everyday activities like baking cookies or playing board games can provide opportunities for siblings to bond. These shared experiences foster a sense of togetherness and create a lasting bond that transcends individual differences.

2. Fostering Cooperation and Teamwork:

Encouraging cooperation and teamwork among siblings is essential for building strong bonds. Parents can involve their children in collaborative projects or activities that require them to work together toward a common goal. This not only teaches valuable life skills but also strengthens the sense of unity among siblings. Whether it's completing a household chore as a team or participating in a school project together, these shared efforts foster a sense of camaraderie and mutual support.

3. Promoting a Sense of Belonging:

Siblings who feel a strong sense of belonging within their family are more likely to develop strong bonds with each other. Parents can cultivate this sense of belonging by emphasizing the importance of family as a source of love and support. Rituals like family dinners, movie nights, or even simple daily check-ins provide opportunities for siblings to connect and reinforce their shared identity as a family.

4. Celebrating Differences:

Each sibling is a unique individual with their own interests, strengths, and weaknesses. Embracing and celebrating these differences is a powerful way to build strong bonds. Encourage siblings to support each other in pursuing their passions and interests. Recognize and celebrate their individual achievements, and teach them that their differences are what make the family tapestry vibrant and diverse.

5. Communication and Empathy:

Effective communication and empathy continue to be vital components in building strong sibling bonds. Encourage siblings to actively listen to each other and validate each other's feelings. Teach them the importance of expressing themselves honestly and respectfully. When conflicts arise, guide them in finding solutions that meet everyone's needs.

When siblings feel heard, understood, and valued, they are more likely to forge lasting connections.

6. Quality Time:

In our fast-paced world, quality time with family can be scarce. However, carving out dedicated time for siblings to connect on a one-on-one basis can be invaluable. These moments allow for deeper conversations, shared interests, and a deeper understanding of each other. Whether it's a sibling outing or a quiet evening at home, these pockets of quality time can be the glue that holds sibling bonds together.

7. Encouraging Mutual Support:

Teaching siblings to be each other's allies and sources of support is a gift that will last a lifetime. Emphasize the importance of being there for one another during both triumphs and challenges. Siblings who know they can count on each other create a network of emotional support that is unmatched by any other relationship.

Building strong bonds among siblings is a continuous process that evolves as they grow and mature. Parents and caregivers play a pivotal role in facilitating these connections by creating an environment that fosters cooperation, celebrates individuality, and promotes open and empathetic communication. Sibling relationships are an enduring treasure, and by investing in their development, we provide our children with companions for life, friends who will be there through thick and thin, and a source of love that stands the test of time.

Nurturing Sibling Relationships That Last a Lifetime

Sibling relationships are unique and enduring, often standing as the longest-lasting connections individuals have in their lives. These bonds have the potential to be a source of unwavering support, companionship, and understanding throughout one's journey from childhood to adulthood. Nurturing sibling relationships that last a lifetime is a gift that can enrich both the individuals involved and the family as a whole

1. **Time and Attention:** Just as any other relationship requires time and attention to flourish, sibling bonds benefit from dedicated moments together. Parents can create opportunities for siblings to spend quality time together, whether through family activities, outings, or simply fostering an environment where siblings can share their thoughts and experiences. These shared moments help build a strong foundation for enduring relationships.

2. **Encouraging Communication**: Effective communication is the linchpin of any healthy relationship. Parents can encourage open and honest dialogue among siblings, emphasizing the importance of active listening and empathy. By teaching children to express their feelings, thoughts, and concerns to each other, parents empower them to develop communication skills that will serve them well throughout their lives.

3. Conflict Resolution Skills: Conflicts are an inevitable part of any relationship, and siblings are no exception. Teaching children how to navigate conflicts in a constructive manner is essential for fostering long-lasting bonds. Conflict resolution skills, such as compromise, negotiation, and understanding differing perspectives, equip siblings with the tools to address disagreements without causing lasting rifts.

4. Celebrating Individuality: Each sibling is a unique individual with their own strengths, interests, and quirks. Parents can promote a sense of acceptance and celebration of these differences, teaching children to appreciate the diverse qualities that make each sibling special. Recognizing and respecting individual identities within the family fosters a sense of belonging and mutual respect.

5. Mutual Support: Sibling relationships can be a powerful source of support throughout life's ups and downs. Encouraging siblings to be each other's cheerleaders, confidants, and allies instills a sense of solidarity that lasts a lifetime. Teaching children that they can rely on each other for emotional support, guidance, and encouragement creates a bond that can weather even the most challenging of circumstances.

6. Family Traditions and Rituals: Establishing family traditions and rituals can be a meaningful way to nurture sibling relationships. Whether it's celebrating birthdays, holidays, or creating unique family traditions, these shared experiences create lasting memories and reinforce the sense of unity within the family.

Nurturing sibling relationships that last a lifetime requires deliberate effort, patience, and a commitment to fostering an environment of love and understanding within the family. These bonds are precious, and by investing in them, parents empower their children with lifelong companions who share their history, their laughter, and their unwavering support. Sibling relationships are a testament to the enduring strength of family, and when nurtured with care, they can stand as a lifelong source of joy and connection.

> **When siblings fight, separating them without taking sides. Taking sides leaves one sibling resentful, waiting for an opportunity to hurt the other.**

CHAPTER FIVE
Parenting Strategies for Nurturing Strong Sibling Relationships

Parenting is a complex and rewarding journey, and one of its most crucial aspects is fostering strong and harmonious sibling relationships. As parents, we play a pivotal role in shaping the dynamics between our children. Implementing effective parenting strategies can empower us to create an environment where siblings not only coexist but thrive together, building bonds that last a lifetime.

1. Setting a Positive Example:

Children learn by example, and parents serve as the primary role models in their lives. Demonstrating respect, empathy, and effective communication within the family sets the tone for how siblings interact with each other. When siblings witness their parents treating each other and other family members with kindness and consideration, they are more likely to emulate these behaviors in their own relationships.

2. Equal Attention and Fairness:

It's essential to ensure that each child feels valued and loved for their unique qualities. While children may have different needs and personalities, parents should strive to provide equal attention and fairness. Recognize and celebrate each child's achievements, no matter how big or small, and avoid making comparisons that can breed jealousy and rivalry.

3. Balancing Individual Needs:

Understanding and meeting the individual needs of each child is vital. While siblings may share common interests, they also have their own passions and pursuits. Encourage and support their individual interests, hobbies, and activities. Balancing these needs allows each child to feel seen and heard within the family.

4. Encouraging Sibling Support:

Foster an environment where siblings are encouraged to support and cheer for each other. Emphasize the importance of being allies, especially during challenging times. Teach them that their siblings are their companions through life's ups and downs. Siblings who feel supported by each other are more likely to develop lasting bonds.

5. Effective Communication with Each Child:

Recognize that each child has their unique communication style and needs. Pay attention to their cues and preferences when it comes to conversation. Some children may be more introverted and prefer one-on-one talks, while others thrive in group settings. Adapt your communication style to suit each child's comfort level, ensuring that they all have opportunities to express themselves.

6. Teaching Conflict Resolution Skills:

Conflict is an inevitable part of any relationship, and sibling bonds are no exception. Teaching children how to resolve conflicts peacefully is a valuable skill. Encourage them to express their feelings and viewpoints while actively listening to their siblings. Guide them in finding solutions that take into account everyone's needs, fostering cooperation rather than competition.

7. **Addressing Favoritism**: Be mindful of unintentional favoritism, which can damage sibling relationships. Ensure that you're not inadvertently showing more attention or favoring one child over another. If you sense any resentment or rivalry brewing, address it openly and honestly, emphasizing your love for each child equally.

8. Family Bonding Time:

Designate regular family bonding time where all members come together for enjoyable activities. These moments can be opportunities for siblings to create shared experiences, collaborate, and have fun together. Family outings, game nights, or simply enjoying meals together can reinforce the sense of togetherness.

9. Encouraging Empathy: Teach children to understand and empathize with their siblings' feelings. Encourage them to put themselves in each other's shoes to gain insight into their emotions and perspectives. Empathy is a powerful tool for building understanding and compassion among siblings.

10. Seeking Professional Help When Necessary:

In some cases, sibling rivalry or conflicts may require professional guidance. If issues persist or escalate to a point where they significantly affect family dynamics, consider seeking the assistance of a family therapist or counselor. These professionals can provide valuable strategies and insights to help siblings overcome challenges.

Nurturing strong sibling relationships requires ongoing effort and dedication, but the rewards are immeasurable. Sibling bonds can be some of the most enduring and cherished relationships in a person's life. By implementing these parenting strategies, we can empower our children to build connections that not only withstand the test of time but also enrich their lives with love, support, and lasting companionship.

> **Accepting that some bickering, fighting and envy are normal and healthy.**

CHAPTER SIX

Sibling Harmony in Practice

The concept of sibling harmony is a beautiful ideal that many parents aspire to achieve within their families. It envisions siblings growing up together, not as adversaries, but as allies, companions, and lifelong friends. While the theory of fostering sibling harmony is essential, its practical application can be both challenging and rewarding. In this exploration, we will delve into practical strategies for turning the vision of sibling harmony into a tangible reality within your family.

1. Real-Life Case Studies:

One of the most effective ways to understand and implement sibling harmony is to study real-life case studies. These can be drawn from your own family experiences or those of others. Examine instances where sibling relationships have thrived and identify the key factors that contributed to their success. Equally valuable are cases where challenges arose – these provide opportunities to learn from mistakes and identify areas for improvement.

2. Practical Exercises and Activities:

To cultivate sibling harmony, consider engaging in practical exercises and activities that encourage cooperation, communication, and bonding. These can range from team-building games and activities to collaborative projects that require siblings to work together. For example, setting up a shared garden or working on a family photo album can be wonderful opportunities for siblings to collaborate and create lasting memories.

3. Monitoring Progress:

Assessing the progress of sibling harmony is crucial to its successful implementation. Keep an open line of communication with your children, asking for their thoughts and feelings about their relationships with their siblings. Encourage them to express any concerns or conflicts they may be experiencing. Regular check-ins allow you to address issues promptly and guide your children toward solutions.

4. Maintaining Positive Dynamics Over Time:

Sibling harmony is not a one-time achievement but an ongoing process. As children grow and their interests evolve, it's essential to adapt your strategies to suit their changing needs. Stay attuned to any shifts in dynamics, and be prepared to intervene when necessary. Encourage your children to continue building their bonds through shared experiences and communication.

5. Fostering Mutual Interests:

Discovering and nurturing mutual interests among siblings can be a powerful catalyst for harmony. Encourage your children to explore common hobbies, sports, or activities that they both enjoy. Whether it's playing a musical instrument, engaging in a sport, or pursuing a shared passion like photography or cooking, shared interests create opportunities for bonding and cooperation.

6. Encouraging Individuality:

While fostering common interests is important, it's equally vital to celebrate and encourage your children's individuality. Each sibling has their unique talents, hobbies, and personalities. Ensure that your children have the freedom to pursue their individual passions and interests, and avoid comparing them to each other. Emphasize that their differences are what make them special and contribute to the richness of your family.

7. Problem-Solving Skills:

Teaching problem-solving skills is invaluable for maintaining sibling harmony. Encourage your children to work together to find solutions to conflicts or challenges that arise. Guide them in brainstorming ideas, evaluating options, and making decisions together. This not only helps resolve immediate issues but also equips them with valuable life skills.

8. Setting Boundaries:

Respect for each other's boundaries is fundamental to sibling harmony. Teach your children the importance of respecting personal space and possessions. Define clear rules and consequences for behavior that invades these boundaries. Ensuring that each child has their safe space and privacy helps minimize conflicts.

9. Encourage Empathy and Understanding:

Empathy is a cornerstone of strong sibling relationships. Encourage your children to develop empathy by helping them understand and appreciate each other's feelings and perspectives. When siblings can empathize with one another, they are more likely to resolve conflicts peacefully and provide emotional support.

10. Family Traditions and Rituals:

Family traditions and rituals provide a sense of unity and create opportunities for siblings to bond. Establishing routines like weekly family dinners, movie nights, or special holiday traditions can become cherished memories that strengthen sibling relationships over time.

In conclusion, sibling harmony is not a mere aspiration but a practical goal that can be achieved through consistent effort, communication, and empathy. By implementing these strategies and adapting them to your family's unique dynamics, you can transform the concept of sibling harmony into a tangible reality within your home. The journey may have its challenges, but the rewards are immeasurable – siblings who not only grow up together but also grow old together as lifelong friends and allies.

Transforming Theory into Reality: Bringing Positive Change to Life

Theory is the seed from which practical change can grow, and the process of turning theory into reality is a powerful journey of transformation. It's the point where ideas, aspirations, and ideals take shape, becoming tangible actions and outcomes. Whether it's achieving personal goals, fostering positive relationships, or making a difference in the world, the art of transforming theory into reality holds the key to progress and growth.

1. Setting Clear Objectives:

The transformation from theory to reality begins with setting clear and achievable objectives. These objectives act as the guiding stars, providing direction and purpose to your endeavors. Whether it's a personal project, a professional goal, or a vision for a better world, defining your objectives is the first step toward making your aspirations a reality.

2. Planning and Strategy:

Once you have your objectives in place, the next crucial step is to create a detailed plan and strategy. This involves breaking down your goals into actionable steps, setting timelines, and allocating resources effectively. A well-thought-out plan not only provides structure but also serves as a roadmap to navigate challenges and uncertainties.

3. Taking Consistent Action:

Transforming theory into reality requires consistent and sustained action. It's about making a commitment to take the necessary steps each day, no matter how small, toward your objectives. Consistency is the fuel that powers progress and turns aspirations into concrete achievements.

4. Embracing Adaptability:

In the journey from theory to reality, it's essential to remain adaptable and open to change. Unexpected obstacles and opportunities may arise, requiring flexibility in your approach. Being willing to adjust your strategies while staying true to your objectives is a key factor in success.

5. Learning and Growth:

Transformation is not only about achieving specific outcomes but also about personal growth and development. Embrace the lessons learned along the way, both from successes and failures. These experiences shape your understanding and refine your strategies, making you better equipped to turn future theories into reality.

6. Patience and Persistence:

Achieving meaningful change often requires patience and persistence. Some goals may take longer to realize than others, and setbacks are a natural part of the process. Maintain your commitment and resilience, recognizing that challenges are stepping stones on the path to transformation.

7. Accountability and Evaluation:

Regularly assess your progress and hold yourself accountable for your actions. Evaluation allows you to measure the effectiveness of your strategies, identify areas for improvement, and make necessary adjustments. It ensures that you stay on track toward turning your theories into concrete results.

8. Celebrating Milestones:

Acknowledge and celebrate your achievements, no matter how small they may seem. Celebrating milestones boosts motivation and reinforces your commitment to transformation. It's a reminder that progress is being made and that your efforts are bearing fruit.

9. Inspiring Others:

The transformation of theory into reality can be a powerful source of inspiration for others. Your actions and accomplishments can serve as a model, motivating and empowering others to pursue their own aspirations and make positive changes in their lives.

10. Sustaining the Momentum:

Once you've turned a theory into reality, the journey doesn't end there. Sustaining the momentum and building upon your achievements is the final phase of transformation. It involves continuous improvement, innovation, and a commitment to ongoing growth and progress.

In conclusion, the art of transforming theory into reality is a dynamic and transformative process that empowers individuals to turn their dreams into tangible outcomes. By setting clear objectives, planning strategically, taking consistent action, and embracing adaptability, individuals can achieve their aspirations and make a meaningful impact on their lives and the world around them. This journey is not only about reaching a destination but also about the growth, learning, and fulfillment that come from the transformational process itself.

The Bad News First...
Your Kids *Really Do* Fight all the Time...

Siblings between 3 and 7 years old engage in some kind of conflict **an average of 3.5 times an hour!**

The first siblings in creation (Cain & Abel) had such conflict it ended in murder.

You can expect your kids will have many conflicts.

CHAPTER SEVEN
Navigating Challenges Along the Way

Sibling rivalry is a common and natural part of growing up with brothers and sisters. While it's not always easy, navigating the challenges of sibling rivalry is crucial for maintaining harmonious family dynamics and fostering strong sibling relationships. In this exploration, we will delve into the various obstacles and strategies for managing sibling rivalry effectively.

1. Understanding the Roots of Rivalry:

To navigate sibling rivalry, it's essential to understand its underlying causes. Sibling rivalry often arises from a desire for parental attention, competition for limited resources (such as toys or privileges), or differences in personality and temperament. Recognizing these root causes can help parents address the specific triggers of rivalry within their family.

2. Equitable Attention and Affection:

One common challenge in managing sibling rivalry is ensuring that each child receives equitable attention and affection. Parents should make a conscious effort to spend quality one-on-one time with each child, acknowledging their individual interests and needs. This practice helps children feel valued and reduces the need to compete for attention.

3. Promoting Effective Communication:

Effective communication is a powerful tool for addressing and preventing conflicts among siblings. Encourage open and empathetic dialogue within the family. Teach children to express their feelings and concerns in a respectful manner. Active listening and validation of emotions can go a long way in diffusing tensions and fostering understanding.

4. Encouraging Cooperation over Competition:

While some level of competition between siblings is normal, parents can guide their children toward a mindset of cooperation over competition. Emphasize the benefits of working together as a team and celebrate joint achievements. Teach them that supporting each other's success ultimately benefits the entire family.

5. Conflict Resolution Skills:

Conflicts are inevitable among siblings. To navigate this challenge, teach children conflict resolution skills. Encourage them to express their grievances constructively, using "I" statements to express their feelings and needs. Provide guidance on how to negotiate and compromise to find mutually acceptable solutions.

6. Avoiding Comparisons:

Avoid making comparisons between siblings, as this can exacerbate rivalry and lead to feelings of inadequacy or jealousy. Each child is unique with their own strengths and weaknesses. Celebrate their individual achievements and emphasize their distinct qualities.

7. Setting Clear Boundaries:

Establishing clear boundaries can help prevent conflicts related to personal space and possessions. Teach children to respect each other's belongings and privacy. Enforce rules consistently and communicate consequences for violating these boundaries.

8. Encouraging Independence:

Encourage each child's independence and autonomy within the family. Allow them to make age-appropriate decisions and choices. Empowering children to have some control over their lives can reduce the need for power struggles with their siblings.

9. Modeling Conflict Resolution:

Parents play a pivotal role in modeling healthy conflict resolution. Demonstrate how to handle disagreements calmly and respectfully in your own interactions. When siblings witness effective conflict resolution between their parents, they are more likely to emulate these skills in their own relationships.

10. Seeking Professional Guidance When Necessary:

In some cases, managing sibling rivalry may require professional guidance. If conflicts persist and significantly disrupt family life, consider seeking the assistance of a family therapist or counselor. These experts can provide specialized strategies and insights to address deeper issues.

11. Patience and Consistency:

Navigating sibling rivalry requires patience and consistency. Changes may not happen overnight, and setbacks are normal. Stay committed to fostering a positive environment and addressing conflicts as they arise. Consistency in applying strategies and setting expectations is key to long-term success.

In conclusion, managing sibling rivalry is a complex but essential aspect of parenting. By understanding the roots of rivalry, promoting effective communication, encouraging cooperation, and teaching conflict resolution skills, parents can navigate the challenges of sibling rivalry effectively. Remember that sibling rivalry is a natural part of growing up, but with guidance and support, siblings can learn to coexist harmoniously and develop strong bonds that last a lifetime.

Dealing with Age Gaps

Navigating age gaps among siblings requires a delicate balance of understanding and inclusivity. Recognize that siblings of different ages often have distinct needs and interests. Encourage older siblings to embrace their role as mentors and protectors, promoting a sense of responsibility and leadership. Younger siblings can benefit from the wisdom and guidance of their older counterparts.

Create opportunities for bonding by engaging in activities that cater to various age groups within the family. Plan family outings, game nights, or shared hobbies that allow siblings to connect on common ground.

Emphasize the importance of inclusion and mutual respect, regardless of age. Encourage open communication where each sibling's voice is heard and valued. Celebrate each child's individuality while fostering a sense of unity within the family.

When approached with patience and understanding, age gaps can transform into bridges that strengthen sibling relationships. Siblings of different ages can learn from each other, building bonds that are diverse, enriching, and enduring.

Handling Sibling Conflict

Handling sibling conflict is a crucial aspect of maintaining a harmonious family environment. Start by promoting open communication, encouraging siblings to express their feelings and concerns respectfully. Teach conflict resolution skills, emphasizing compromise and finding solutions that satisfy all parties involved. Set clear boundaries and consequences for inappropriate behavior, ensuring consistency in enforcement. Model conflict resolution through your own interactions, showing how disagreements can be handled calmly and respectfully. Encourage siblings to see each other's perspectives and practice empathy. Ultimately, sibling conflict can be an opportunity for growth, teaching valuable life skills and strengthening sibling bonds when resolved constructively.

Addressing Individual Needs

Addressing individual needs is essential when managing sibling rivalry. Each child within the family has unique interests, strengths, and developmental stages. Parents should recognize and celebrate these differences, ensuring that each child feels valued for their individual qualities.

Encourage children to pursue their passions and interests, even if they differ from their siblings'. This fosters a sense of autonomy and self-esteem. Allocate one-on-one time with each child to cater to their specific needs, whether it's helping with homework, engaging in a hobby, or simply having a meaningful conversation.

By addressing individual needs, parents reduce the competition for attention and resources, thus mitigating the triggers of rivalry. It reinforces to each child that they are loved and supported for who they are, promoting a healthier family dynamic and stronger sibling relationships.

CHAPTER EIGHT

The Lifelong Benefits of Strong Sibling Bonds

In this final chapter, we embark on a journey that explores the enduring and profound advantages of nurturing strong sibling bonds that persist well into adulthood. These relationships, forged in the crucible of family, provide a foundation for emotional support, companionship, and the transmission of core values across generations. Let's delve into the lifelong benefits that strong sibling bonds bring to our lives.

Sibling Bonds in Adulthood:

As we transition from childhood into adulthood, our relationships with siblings often mature and transform. While childhood may have been marked by playful rivalry and shared secrets, adulthood brings a deeper level of connection. Adult siblings frequently become each other's confidants, advisors, and trusted companions. These bonds are grounded in the knowledge that someone who has known us since birth stands by our side, offering unwavering support.

In this section, we'll explore the evolution of sibling relationships as we grow older. We'll discuss the unique roles that adult siblings play in each other's lives, from offering emotional solace during challenging times to celebrating achievements and milestones. We'll also touch upon the ways adult siblings can foster a sense of belonging and continuity, helping us navigate the complexities of life in the company of those who share our history.

Supporting Each Other Through Life's Challenges:

Life is an unpredictable journey, marked by joys and tribulations. Having strong sibling bonds can be an immeasurable asset when confronting life's challenges. Whether we're grappling with the loss of a loved one, navigating career transitions, or facing personal crises, siblings often serve as an anchor in the storm. Their unwavering support, understanding, and shared history provide a unique source of solace and strength.

In this section, we'll delve into real-life stories that exemplify the profound support siblings offer one another during life's trials. We'll witness how sibling bonds can ease the burdens of adversity, offer practical assistance, and provide an emotional refuge. These narratives illustrate the incredible power of familial relationships in times of need, highlighting the lasting impact of strong sibling connections in adulthood.

Passing Down Strong Values to Future Generations:

Sibling bonds are not confined to the individuals involved; they extend their influence to future generations. Families with strong sibling relationships often cultivate a culture founded on empathy, cooperation, and mutual respect. These values are transmitted from one generation to the next, leaving an indelible mark on family dynamics and relationships.

In this final section, we'll explore how adult siblings collaborate to instill these vital values in their own children. We'll witness how the lessons learned from strong sibling bonds shape the way families interact, communicate, and support each other. These shared values create a legacy that endures, perpetuating the tradition of close-knit family bonds for generations to come.

In conclusion, the benefits of fostering strong sibling bonds reach far beyond childhood. These relationships evolve and mature with us, becoming vital sources of love, companionship, and support throughout our lives. As we navigate the challenges of adulthood, our siblings stand as steadfast allies, enriching our experiences and enhancing our emotional well-being.

Moreover, the values cultivated through strong sibling bonds have a ripple effect, touching the lives of future generations. The empathy, cooperation, and respect nurtured within these relationships become cornerstones of family culture, fostering a sense of unity and connectedness that endures across time.

As we close this chapter and this exploration of the lifelong benefits of strong sibling bonds, we are reminded of the profound impact these relationships have on our individual journeys and the collective tapestry of our families. By cherishing and nurturing these bonds, we not only enrich our own lives but also contribute to a world where love, understanding, and support are cherished across generations.

CONCLUSION

As we conclude this exploration of sibling relationships, we find ourselves at the threshold of an exciting journey ahead—a journey characterized by the pursuit of harmonious family dynamics and enduring sibling bonds. We've delved into the complexities and nuances of these relationships, understanding that they are a cornerstone of our lives, with implications reaching far beyond childhood.

Throughout this journey, we've uncovered essential insights into the importance of fostering strong sibling bonds from an early age. We've learned that these bonds provide a foundation of trust, support, and companionship that shape our growth, development, and well-being. From navigating sibling rivalry to celebrating the lifelong benefits of these connections, we've seen the profound impact that siblings have on our lives.

As we move forward, we must recognize that the journey does not end here. It continues as we apply the knowledge and strategies gleaned from this exploration to our own families. It extends to the nurturing of our children's sibling relationships, ensuring that they too can experience the enduring benefits of strong bonds.

Embracing a harmonious family future requires dedication, communication, and empathy. It involves recognizing and addressing the unique needs and challenges of each family member while fostering an environment of love and understanding. It means celebrating the differences that make each sibling special and unique.

We'll have the opportunity to put these insights into practice, cultivating strong sibling bonds and creating a legacy of love, support, and unity within our families. The journey may have its challenges, but the rewards are immeasurable—a harmonious family future where siblings grow old together as lifelong friends and allies, enriching each other's lives and contributing to a brighter world.

So, let us embark on this journey with open hearts and open minds, embracing the promise of harmonious sibling relationships and the boundless potential they hold for our families and generations to come.

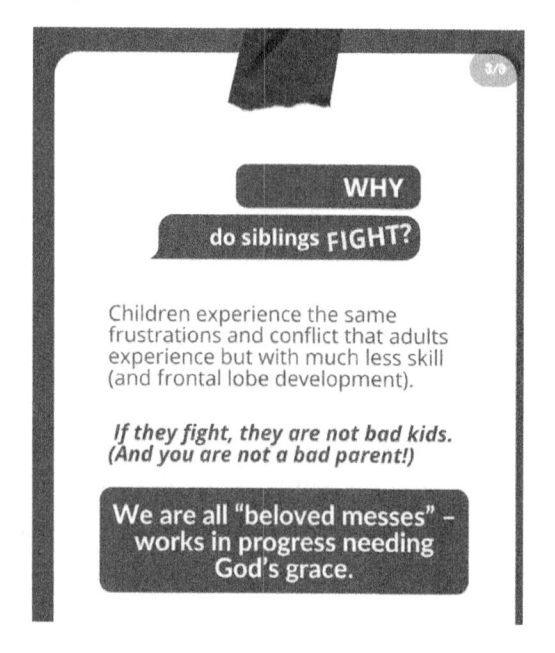

> **WHY do siblings FIGHT?**
>
> Children experience the same frustrations and conflict that adults experience but with much less skill (and frontal lobe development).
>
> *If they fight, they are not bad kids. (And you are not a bad parent!)*
>
> We are all "beloved messes" – works in progress needing God's grace.

Made in United States
North Haven, CT
05 September 2025